Everyday Heroes

Firefighters

Jill Wheeler
ABDO Publishing Company

visit us at
www.abdopub.com

Published by ABDO Publishing Company, 4940 Viking Drive, Edina, Minnesota 55435.
Copyright © 2003 by Abdo Consulting Group, Inc. International copyrights reserved in all
countries. No part of this book may be reproduced in any form without written permission from
the publisher.

Printed in the United States.

Editors: Kate A. Conley, Kristy Langanki Cannon, Kristianne E. Vieregger
Photo Credits: AP/Wide World, Corbis
Art Direction: Neil Klinepier

Library of Congress Cataloging-in-Publication Data

Wheeler, Jill C., 1964-
    Firefighters / Jill C. Wheeler.
      p. cm. -- (Everyday heroes)
    Includes index.
    Summary: An overview of the occupation of firefighting, including an historical
perspective, the training needed, and the work done, and also including tips on
preventing fires.
    ISBN 1-57765-855-8
    1. Fire extinction--Juvenile literature. 2. Fire fighters--Juvenile literature. [1. Fire
fighters. 2. Fire extinction. 3. Occupations.] I. Title. II. Everyday heroes (Edina, Minn.)

TH9148 .W44 2002
628.9'25'092--dc21
                                   2002025364

Contents

Firefighters 4

Humble Beginnings 6

Passing the Test 10

It Takes a Team 12

A Firefighter's Gear 16

Fire Trucks 18

Other Emergencies 20

Back at the Station............................24

A Job Worth Doing.............................26

Help the Helpers 28

Glossary 30

Web Sites 31

Index 32

Firefighters

Every day, firefighters race to emergencies. These men and women risk their lives to put out fires and rescue people. They are true heroes in their communities.

Some firefighters are volunteers. They are not paid for their work. Other firefighters are professionals. Fighting fires and helping others is their job.

Firefighters work in small towns and large cities all over the world. Some firefighters tackle forest fires. Others **extinguish** fires at airports and on airplanes. Still others put out fires in oil fields or on ships.

Firefighters serve their communities in other ways, too. Firefighters often help accident victims. They rescue people who are trapped. In addition, they teach people about fire prevention and fire safety.

A firefighter's job is not easy. It takes courage, strength, and intelligence to fight fires and rescue people. Though the job can be difficult, it can also be rewarding.

Firefighters risk their lives to save others.

Humble Beginnings

Early American colonists did not have special forces for fighting fires. Instead, everyone worked together to battle blazes. To do this, they formed bucket **brigades**.

When a fire started, people grabbed their buckets. Then they formed two lines. The lines stretched from the fire to a water source. One line passed buckets full of water to people fighting the fire. The other line passed the empty buckets back to be refilled.

Bucket brigades didn't always stop the fires. Sometimes the fires just grew bigger. Fires often destroyed entire towns. People could only stand by and watch.

In 1648, the leader of present-day New York City, New York, appointed fire **wardens**. The fire wardens inspected chimneys for fire **hazards**. This was one of the first fire prevention efforts in the colonies.

Opposite page: People in the New York Colony put out a fire with buckets and a hand pump in 1733.

Later, city leaders appointed eight citizens as patrols. The patrols walked the streets at night. If they saw a fire, they shook wooden rattles to warn people. This was one of the first attempts at organized fire fighting in the colonies.

Slowly, fire fighting continued to improve. In 1679, the first paid fire department in the colonies was formed in Boston, Massachusetts. In 1736, Benjamin Franklin founded the Union Fire Company in Philadelphia, Pennsylvania. It became the model for volunteer fire-fighting forces.

Communities soon became more involved in fire fighting. They made rules to prevent fires and created better fire-fighting equipment. They also formed fire departments. Many of the firefighters were volunteers.

Today, most fire departments are a part of local governments. Fire departments from different cities work together to fight big fires.

Some firefighters work for the federal government. They often battle forest fires. Some U.S. soldiers work as firefighters for the military. Any of these firefighters may join with local forces to save lives and property.

Horses pulled fire trucks during the mid-1800s and early 1900s. Steam engines powered the water pumps.

Federal **agencies** may also work with local fire departments to investigate what caused a fire. Agents from the Federal Bureau of Investigation (FBI) can help. So can Certified Fire Investigators (CFIs). CFIs work for the federal Bureau of Alcohol, Tobacco, and Firearms.

The U.S. military employs about 2,000 firefighters. They often work at military bases.

Passing the Test

What does it take to be a firefighter? Firefighters must be physically fit. They need to be calm, focused, and alert. They must work well with others. And they must be willing to risk their own lives to save others.

People who want to be firefighters must have a high school education. They must also pass written, spoken, and physical tests.

The physical test is challenging. Candidates wear heavy fire-fighting gear and perform several tasks. They drag, carry, and roll up heavy hoses. They climb walls and drag dummies to safety. They also carry and position long ladders. Candidates must finish this test within a given amount of time in order to pass.

Candidates who pass all the tests are placed on **probation** with a fire department. The department sends them to training where they learn fire-fighting skills. Then they begin working. When the **probation** period has ended, firefighters receive a permanent job.

Good firefighters are always learning. They can take classes to become **Emergency Medical Technicians (EMTs)** or get other advanced training. That way, they can handle many different kinds of emergencies.

This candidate drags a 200-pound (91-kg) dummy for 100 feet (30 m) during his physical skills test.

It Takes a Team

A firefighter's first job is to rescue anyone who might be in danger. Firefighters look for people and animals as soon as they arrive at a fire.

Everyone in a fire department has an important job.

Next, they confine the fire and put out the flames. To do this, they use hoses to spray water on the fire. They also open doors, break windows, and cut holes in the roof. Doing this helps smoke and heat escape.

Once the fire is **extinguished**, firefighters inspect the area. They want to make sure they have put out any hidden **embers** or flames.

To accomplish these tasks, firefighters must work as a team. Team members have different jobs. The fire chief manages the entire fire department. He or she also directs firefighters during large fires.

The **apparatus** operator is another team member. He or she drives the fire truck, which firefighters call an apparatus. The driver also maintains the truck and operates its pumps and ladders. Drivers are also called engineers or **chauffeurs**.

Several firefighters must work as a team to control the hose and put out the flames.

Hazardous materials (hazmat) specialists are also team members. They have special training on how to handle hazardous fires. For example, using water would spread a gasoline fire. So hazmat specialists use a foam spray to put out gasoline fires. They wear special gear for protection.

Not all team members race to the fire. Fire departments need office workers, too. Office employees do their part by keeping the fire station operating smoothly.

One of the most important office employees is the dispatcher. Fire department dispatchers receive fire emergency calls from **911 call centers**. Then they decide which people and equipment to send to the emergency.

Some fire departments also have investigators. They determine how a fire started. To do this, investigators sift through the ashes for evidence. They also investigate fires they think may have been set on purpose.

Setting a fire on purpose is called arson. It is a serious crime. If investigators suspect arson, they may send evidence to a laboratory. Laboratories that help with criminal investigations are called forensic science laboratories.

Computers in a fire department's control room are important. They allow dispatchers to see which people and equipment are at the station, at the scene of an emergency, or on the way there.

15

A Firefighter's Gear

For a firefighter, rescuing people often means running into a burning, smoky building. To protect themselves, firefighters wear turnout gear. Turnout gear has many parts.

Helmets protect firefighters from heat, chemicals, and falling materials. The helmet includes a face shield. A fireproof hood beneath the helmet protects a firefighter's ears and neck. Heavy boots protect a firefighter's feet.

An SCBA air tank

Firefighters also wear coats, gloves, and **bunker pants** made from fireproof fabric. They protect firefighters from heat and flames. Bunker pants are very heavy. They weigh nearly four pounds (2 kg)!

To avoid breathing smoke, firefighters use a self-contained breathing **apparatus** (SCBA). SCBAs have an air tank and a mask. They provide firefighters with 15 to 30 minutes of fresh air.

Some firefighters carry a personal alert safety system. It senses motion. If a firefighter stops moving, an alarm sounds. This calls the other firefighters to come help.

Firefighters carry other tools, too. Axes break down doors and shatter windows. Ropes are used to rescue people and help firefighters escape. Firefighters also use radios to talk to each other.

Firefighters help each other put on their gear during a practice session.

Fire Trucks

Trucks transport firefighters to emergencies. They also help firefighters rescue victims and put out fires. Firefighters use three main kinds of trucks. They are pumper trucks, ladder trucks, and rescue trucks.

Three to six firefighters operate a pumper truck. These trucks have pumps built into them. They pump water into the fire-fighting hoses.

Firefighters use a ladder truck to enter the upper floor of a burning building.

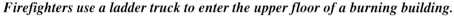

A pumper truck can pump water from fire **hydrants**, lakes, ponds, and even pools! It can also pump water from its tank. The tank may hold 500 gallons (1,900 liters) of water. A pumper truck also carries extra hoses, **nozzles**, and ladders.

Firefighters use ladder trucks, too. A heavy-duty ladder is attached to the truck's frame. The truck's engine powers this ladder. It can extend up to 100 feet (30 m).

Firefighters use ladder trucks to rescue people in tall buildings. They also use ladder trucks to reach fires that are several stories up. Three to eight firefighters operate the ladder truck.

Rescue trucks carry tools to help firefighters. Rams are sturdy poles that hold up floors in a burning building. Air guns slice through metal to create escape hatches. Cutters and the Jaws of Life cut and **pry** apart twisted metal. **Jacks** can lift heavy objects off trapped people.

A firefighter connects a hose to a pumper truck.

Other Emergencies

Firefighters do more in a day than fight fires. They also respond to other emergencies. Some firefighters are also **EMTs**. They have special medical training.

Some fire departments have an **ambulance**. The ambulance and fire truck may race off together. Firefighters often reach accident scenes before other emergency workers.

Firefighters are accustomed to helping car crash victims. They sometimes go to the homes of sick people, too. They can care for those people until other medical help arrives.

Some emergencies involve search and rescue. They can be simple jobs, such as freeing a child locked in his or her house. Or they can be complicated jobs. Firefighters may have to crawl through collapsed buildings looking for survivors.

Firefighters also help during natural **disasters**. They can search for people trapped after tornadoes, hurricanes, and earthquakes. Firefighters often use trained dogs to help find survivors.

Firefighters use rescue dogs to search for survivors after the terrorist attack on the World Trade Center on September 11, 2001.

Firefighters can also help with water rescues. Some firefighters are divers who can rescue people under water. They also save people who are trapped by rising flood waters. They can rescue people who have fallen through thin ice, too.

Once firefighters rescue people, they take them to a waiting **ambulance**. The ambulance works like a small emergency room. If a firefighter gets hurt, the ambulance can be used to treat him or her as well.

In addition to rescuing people and fighting fires, firefighters do other activities. These may be less exciting than fighting fires. But they are necessary for the community's health and safety.

One of these activities is fire prevention. Firefighters inspect public buildings to find possible fire **hazards**. They also visit schools to teach students about fire safety.

Firefighters spend time sharpening their skills, too. They practice fighting fires and rescuing people. They exercise to stay fit and take classes to learn new skills. They also make sure their equipment works perfectly.

A firefighter teaches a student about fire fighting during a fire safety program (above). Firefighters practice their skills during a drill at an abandoned building (right).

Back at the Station

Fire stations are the center of the fire-fighting force. Fire departments in large cities have several fire stations. They are placed throughout the city. There may be a fire station to serve each neighborhood.

Fire stations are much like houses. Firefighters live there during their 24-hour shifts. Fire stations have laundry rooms, workout rooms, and kitchens. They have large garages for the fire and rescue trucks, too.

Fire stations also have places for firefighters to sleep. Firefighters are not always at an emergency. So they may get a normal night's sleep during their shift. On a busy night, they may not get any sleep at all.

On-duty firefighters are at the station throughout their shift. They leave the station to respond to emergencies. They may work alongside **EMTs** or other emergency workers.

The fire station is a second home for firefighters. When not responding to emergencies, firefighters often enjoy joking with each other and eating meals together.

A Job Worth Doing

Fighting fires is difficult work. Firefighters also are at high risk of being hurt on the job. So why do so many firefighters love their work?

Some firefighters like the challenge. They never know what each day will bring. They also enjoy the thrill of danger.

Firefighters are proud to help.

Other firefighters like helping people. They are proud to make a difference in their communities.

Some firefighters choose to carry on a family tradition. Many of them have fathers or other relatives who have worked as firefighters. They are proud of this **heritage**.

Other firefighters like the job's lifestyle. Professional firefighters often work in 24-hour shifts. They work 24 hours and then have two or three days off.

Volunteer firefighters are not paid for their work. Professional firefighters are paid. Their salaries come from tax money. Professional firefighters also receive insurance.

A firefighter's bravery and skill keep the community safe.

Help the Helpers

You can help your local firefighters. Learn how to prevent fires and know what to do if a fire occurs. Encourage your family members to do the same.

- Look around your house for fire **hazards**. Hazards include outlets overloaded with cords, space heaters that are too close to curtains or furniture, and **flammable** items stored near heat sources. Talk to an adult about fixing these hazards.

- If you're in a burning building, walk calmly to the fire escape. If you're in a smoky room, crawl to safety. The air is better near the ground. If your clothes catch on fire, stop, drop, and roll to put it out. Never go back into a burning building. Tell the firefighters if someone is still inside.

- Make sure your home has a fire **extinguisher** and learn how to use it. Make sure your home has a working smoke alarm, too.

28

- Don't play with matches. Never leave a candle or fireplace burning without someone to watch it.

- Never sound a false fire alarm. If you really do see a fire, sound the alarm or call 911. Tell an adult right away if you or a friend accidentally starts a fire.

- Hold a practice fire drill with your family. Decide on a meeting place outside your house. Tell everyone to go there if a fire happens. That way you can quickly see if your whole family is safe.

People of all ages can help prevent fires.

Glossary

agency - a department of the government.

ambulance - an automobile that carries sick or injured people.

apparatus - equipment designed for a specific purpose.

brigade - a group of people who are organized to perform a specific task.

bunker pants - pants made of fireproof material.

chauffeur - a person who drives a fire truck or another automobile.

disaster - an event that causes suffering or loss of life. Natural disasters include events such as hurricanes, tornadoes, and earthquakes.

ember - a particle from a fire that is still glowing with heat.

Emergency Medical Technician (EMT) - a person who is medically trained to assist patients at the scene of an emergency.

extinguish - to put out a fire.

flammable - easily set on fire.

hazard - a source of danger.

heritage - something handed down from one generation to the next.

hydrant - a pipe with a spout from which water may be drawn.

jack - a device used for raising heavy objects.

911 call center - a central location for answering 911 phone calls.

nozzle - the tip on a hose.

probation - a period of time during which a person is evaluated.

pry - to pull apart.

warden - a person who is in charge of something.

Web Sites

Would you like to learn more about firefighters? Please visit **www.abdopub.com** to find up-to-date Web site links about becoming a firefighter, as well as tips for fire safety and fire prevention. These links are routinely monitored and updated to provide the most current information available.

Firefighters perform their jobs with courage and strength.

Index

A

ambulances 20, 22
apparatus operator 13
arson 14

B

Boston, Massachusetts 8
bucket brigades 6
Bureau of Alcohol,
    Tobacco, and
    Firearms 9

C

Certified Fire
    Investigators 9

D

dispatchers 14

E

Emergency Medical
    Technicians 11, 20,
    24
equipment 8, 10, 12, 13,
    14, 17, 18, 19, 22

F

Federal Bureau of
    Investigation 9
fire chief 12
firefighters, professional
    4, 8, 26, 27
firefighters, volunteer 4,
    8, 27
fire hazards 6, 22, 28, 29
fire prevention 4, 6, 8, 22,
    28, 29
fire safety 4, 22, 28, 29
fire station 14, 24
fire trucks 13, 18, 19, 20,
    24
forensic science
    laboratories 14
Franklin, Benjamin 8
funding 27

G

gear 10, 14, 16, 17

H

hazardous materials
    specialists 14

I

investigators 9, 14

J

job duties 4, 8, 12, 13, 14,
    20, 22

L

ladder trucks 18, 19

N

New York City, New York
    6, 7

P

Philadelphia,
    Pennsylvania 8
pumper trucks 18, 19

R

rescue trucks 18, 19, 24
rescue work 4, 12, 16, 18,
    19, 20, 22

T

tests 10
training 10, 11, 20, 22